stitchwort

bachelor's
buttons

tansy

fennel

daisy

First Published in 1970 by
Macdonald and Company
(Publishers) Limited
St. Giles House
49-50 Poland Street
London W1

Managing Editor
Michael W. Dempsey B.A.

Chief Editor
Angela Sheehan B.A.

Made and printed in Great Britain
by A. Wheaton & Company
Exeter Devon

MACDONALD FIRST LIBRARY

# How Flowers Live

Macdonald Educational
49-50 Poland Street
London W1

Plants with flowers grow everywhere.
They grow in gardens, in fields and in
hedgerows.
Some trees have flowers.
Weeds have flowers.
Even cabbages have flowers.
Some plants, such as toadstools, ferns and
pine trees, do not have flowers.

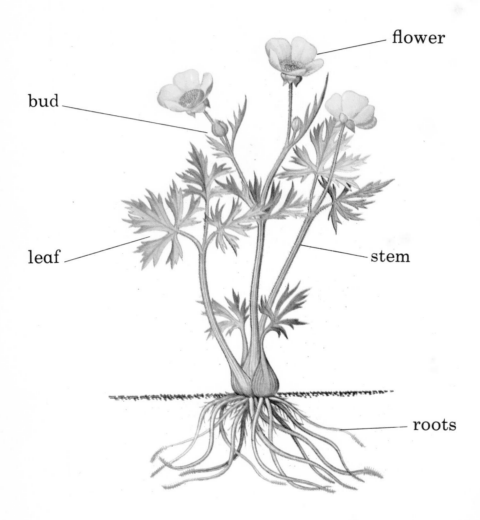

flower

bud

leaf

stem

roots

All plants with flowers have roots that grow
down into the soil.

All plants have stems.
The stems grow upwards into the
air and towards the light.

On the stems are the leaves and flowers.
The leaves are green.

The young leaves and flowers are the buds.

Each part of the plant does a special job.

Roots keep the plant firmly in the ground.
They stop winds blowing the plant over.
They stop animals pulling the plant out of
the ground.
The roots also take in water from the soil.
There are important minerals in the water.

There are two kinds of root.
One kind is a long thick root.
It is called a tap-root.
Plants store food in this kind of root.
Thistles and dandelions have tap-roots.
The other kind of root has many branches.
It is called a fibrous root.
Most garden flowers have fibrous roots.

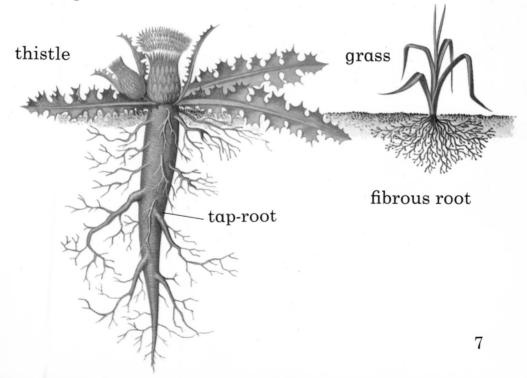

thistle

grass

tap-root

fibrous root

food — water

Inside the stem of a
plant, there are many
tubes.
The tubes carry
water and food
to all parts of the plant.

Wood is made of
many of these tubes.

The stem also
supports the leaves
and flowers.

Trees need strong stems
to carry all the
branches and leaves.

Their stems are made of
wood.
You can tell the age of
a tree by counting the
rings of wood.
Each ring is one year's
growth.

9

Leaves also have tubes in them.
They are called veins.
The veins in the leaf are joined to the tubes
in the stem.
If you put a leaf stalk into an ink-well,
you will see the ink going up the veins.
This is how water reaches every part of a
leaf.

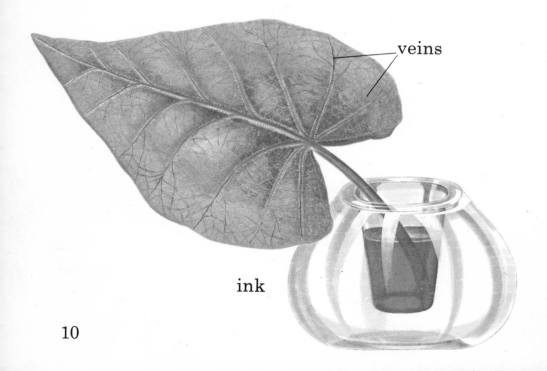

veins

ink

All these leaves have different shapes.
You can often know a plant by the shape of its
leaves.

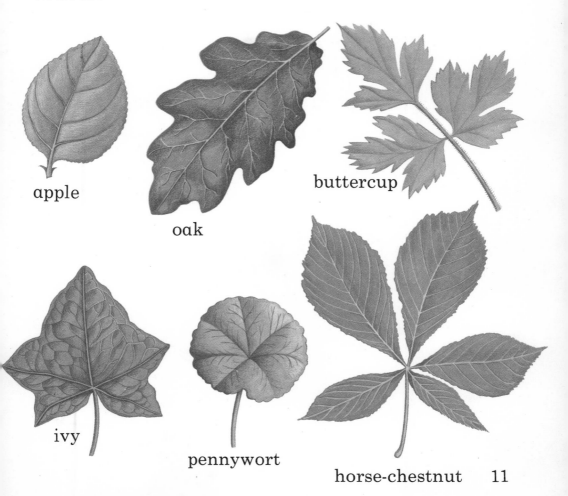

apple

oak

buttercup

ivy

pennywort

horse-chestnut 11

Leaves make food for the plant.
To make food they need water and a special
gas from the air, called carbon-dioxide.
They also need sunshine.

There is a special green stuff in the
leaves which uses the sunshine to turn the
water and the gas into food.
The green stuff is called chlorophyll.
Plants do not grow well in shady places.
There is not enough sunshine for the leaves
to make very much food.

13

This is a buttercup flower.
Some of the petals have been taken away to
show all the parts.

On the outside there are green sepals.
These protect the flower when it is a
young bud.

A buttercup has five yellow petals.
At the bottom of each petal is a part that
makes sweet nectar for insects.

Inside the petals there are many stamens.
Pollen is made at the top of each stamen.

In the middle of the flower are the carpels.
At the bottom of each carpel is a seed-box.
This is where the young seeds develop.

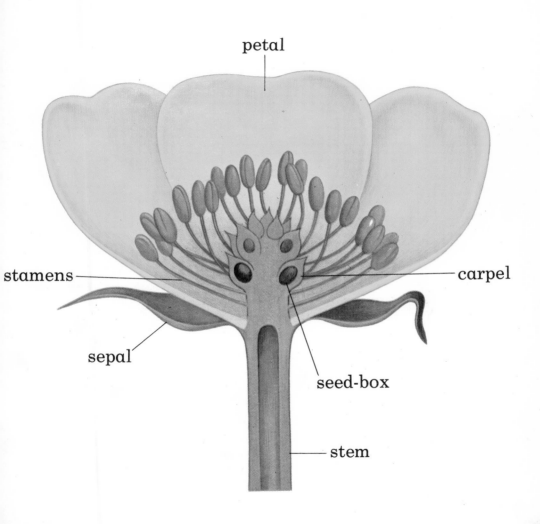

petal

stamens

carpel

seed-box

sepal

stem

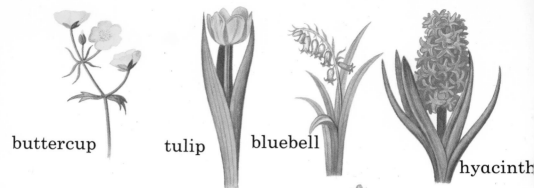

buttercup    tulip    bluebell

hyacinth

Some plants, such as
tulips, have only one
flower at the top of their
stems.
Some plants have more
than one flower on
each stem.
A bluebell has several
flowers hanging like
bells from its stem.
Other plants have clusters
of flowers on their stems.

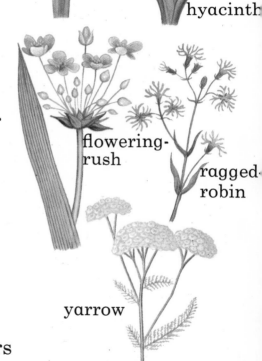

flowering-
rush

ragged-
robin

yarrow

16

dandelion

flower

The flower on a dandelion or thistle plant
is not really one flower.
It is hundreds of very small flowers together.
Daisies are just the same.
This family of flowers is the biggest in
the world.

flower

thistle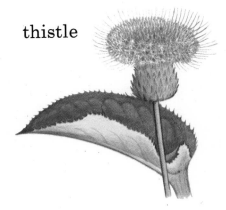

Flowers make seeds from
which new plants grow.
Before a flower can
make seeds it must be
brushed with pollen from
another flower.
This is called pollination.

Sometimes the pollen is
carried from one flower
to another by insects.

Insects do not mean to pollinate flowers.
They visit brightly coloured flowers to
feed on the nectar at the bottom of the petals.
As they reach into the flowers pollen clings
to their bodies.
As they move from flower to flower the pollen
is brushed onto the carpels.

Most grasses and trees do not have bright
petals and nectar to attract insects.
Their pollen is blown by the wind.

pollen
'basket'

This bee is putting pollen from a sweet-pea
flower into 'baskets' on its legs.
It carries the pollen home to feed its young.
On the way home it may visit other sweet-pea
flowers and pollinate them.

20

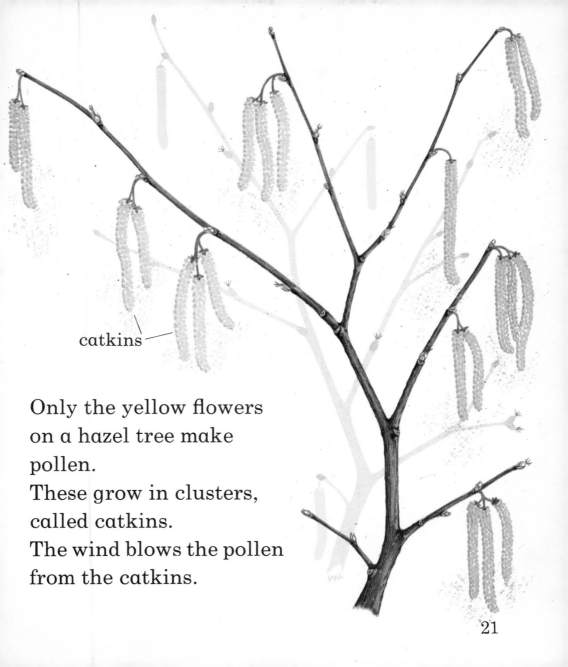

catkins

Only the yellow flowers
on a hazel tree make
pollen.
These grow in clusters,
called catkins.
The wind blows the pollen
from the catkins.

buttercup

carpels

ripe fruits

seeds

When a flower is pollinated, the seeds begin
to grow in the seed box.
The carpels grow into fruits which cover the
seeds and protect them.

Different plants have different fruits.
Some fruits are hard, like those of the poppy.
Some fruits are fleshy, like those of the
tomato.

# These are all fruits.

oats

strawberry

blackberry

horse-chestnut

pea

poppy

tomato

bean

rose

apple

23

When the fruits and seeds are ripe they fall
from the plant.

poppy

The seeds of the poppy
are shaken from holes
in the fruits by the wind.
The seeds of the
snapdragon are also
shaken from the fruits.

snapdragon

The fruits of the violet
and the stock dry and
split open.
This flicks the seeds
onto the ground.

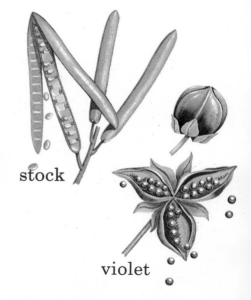

stock

violet

24

Dandelion and thistle
fruits have hairy
parachutes.
The wind carries
them for miles.

Sycamore and lime fruits
have wings.
They can glide through
the air for a long way.

dandelion

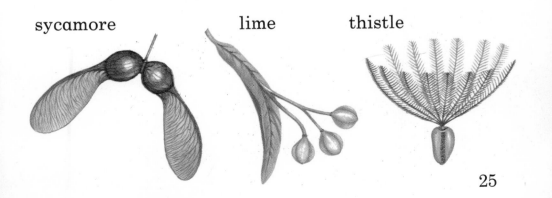

sycamore          lime          thistle

25

Some fruits are carried away by animals.
Birds eat mistletoe berries and squirrels
eat acorns.
Ants take home seeds to feed their young.
Sometimes animals drop the fruits or seeds
on the ground.
Then a new plant can grow.
Prickly burrs stick to the fur of animals.
They may be carried a long way before they
drop to the ground.

The fruits of the water-lily are full of air bubbles.
They float away on the water.

spongy fruit

water-lily

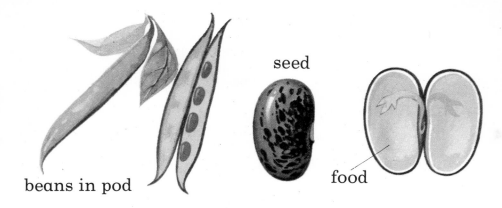

seed

food

beans in pod

Inside every seed is a small plant with lots of food around it.

The plant grows as it feeds on the food. You can watch a bean grow if you put it between blotting-paper and the side of a jam-jar. You must keep the paper wet.

28

After a few days, the
hard shell of the seed
splits.
Out comes a small root.
This grows downwards.

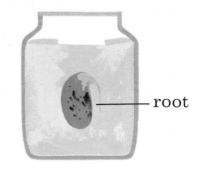

root

Then a small stem grows
from the seed.
It has leaves at the
top.
The stem grows upwards.

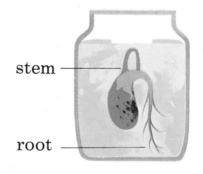

stem

root

The root and stem keep
on growing.
The root grows side-roots.
The plant is now a
seedling.

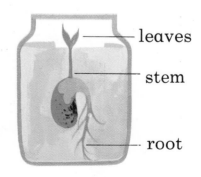

leaves

stem

root

The bean seedling has now used up all the food in the seed.
The seedling must be put in the soil so that it can grow bigger.
From the soil it can take in water and minerals for its leaves to make food.
The soil must be firmly pressed round the roots.
The plant must be watered for a few days.

The bean plant lives
for only one year,
so it must grow very
quickly and make seeds
by the end of the summer.

The flowers are
pollinated by insects.
The seeds grow and ripen
in the pods.

When the pods are ripe,
we can pick the seeds
and grow new plants
from them.

31

# Index

Buttercup, 4, 5, 8, 14, 15, 16, 22

Carpels, 14, 15, 19, 22
Chlorophyll, 12

Fibrous root, 7
Flower, 14, 15
Fruits, 22, 25

Insect pollination, 18, 19, 20

Leaves, 10, 11

Nectar, 14

Petals, 14, 15
Pollination, 18-21

Roots, 6, 7

Seed-box, 14, 15, 22
Seeds, 22-29
Sepals, 14, 15
Stamens, 14, 15
Stem, 8, 9

Tap-root, 7

Water dispersal, 27
Wind pollination, 21
Wood, 8, 9

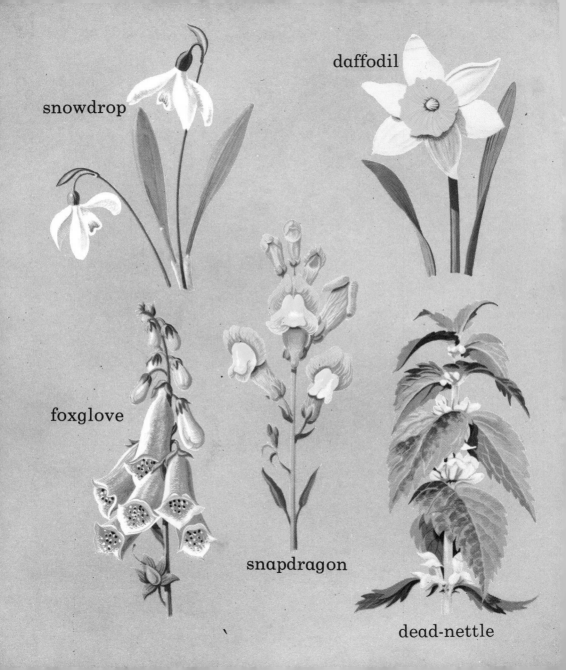

snowdrop

daffodil

foxglove

snapdragon

dead-nettle